SONGS FOR SIGHT-SINGING

High School — Tenor-Bass

Compiled by
Mary Henry and Maril

Consulting Editor
Dr. Ruth Whitlock

Director of Music Education Studies
Texas Christian University

SOUTHERN MUSIC COMPANY
Publishing Division

B-371

TABLE OF CONTENTS

B-371

PREFACE

SONGS FOR SIGHT SINGING provides a collection of literature for use in the choral classroom. Each selection was composed according to criteria designed by Texas secondary choral directors and commissioned by the Texas University Interscholastic League for use in its annual sight singing contest. These graded materials were created specifically for young musicians by recognized composers and comprise a valuable resource as they contain many of the problems encountered in sight singing. This collection can be used effectively as a supplement to the daily instructional sight singing program after an approved system (movable "do", fixed "do" or numbers) and a rhythm system are established within the choral curriculum.

NOAH'S ARK

(TT*, TTB, TB*, TBB)

American Black Spiritual
Arranged by BOBBY L. SILTMAN

Tenor I

Tenor II

or

Baritone

Bass

Piano

There's one,_____ Just one more riv-er to cross._____

There's one,_____ Just one more riv-er to cross._____ Old

There's one,_____ Just one more riv-er to cross._____ Old

There's one, Just one more riv-er to cross._____ Old

There's one more riv-er to

No-ah built him-self an ark, There's one more riv-er to

No-ah built him-self an ark, There's one more riv-er to

No-ah built him-self an ark, There's one more riv-er to

* This selection may be sung without the bass part.

6

Ar - a - rat There's one more riv - er to cross.

Ar - a - rat There's one more riv - er to cross.

Ar - a - rat There's one more riv - er to cross.

There's one more riv - er to cross.

One more riv - er, There's one more riv - er to Jor - don.

One more riv - er, There's one more riv - er to Jor - don.

One more riv - er, There's one more riv - er to Jor - don.

One more riv - er, There's one more riv - er to Jor - don.

One more riv - er, There's one more riv - er to cross._____ There's

One more riv - er, There's one more riv - er to cross._____ There's

One more riv - er, There's one more riv - er to cross._____ There's

One more riv - er, There's one more riv - er to cross._____

one,_____ Just one more riv - er to cross._____

one,_____ Just one more riv - er to cross._____

one,_____ Just one more riv - er to cross._____

Just one Just one more riv - er to cross._____

ALLELUIA
(TTB or TBB)*

American Black Spiritual
Arranged by BOBBY L. SILTMAN

*Key may be raised to F major for younger male voices.

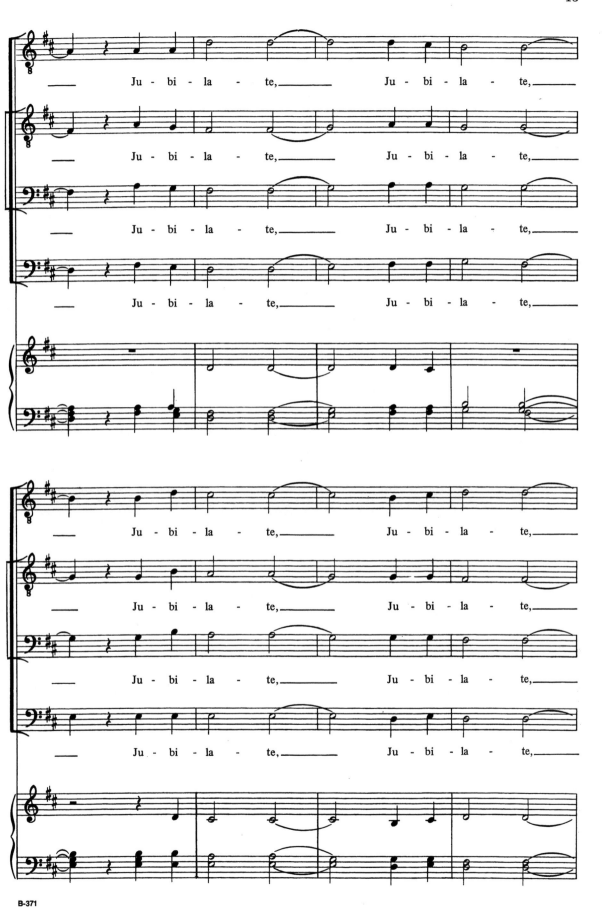

14

GOODBYE, MY LOVER, GOODBYE

(TT*, TTB, TB*, or TBB)

Sea Chantey
Arranged by BOBBY L. SILTMAN

*This selection may be sung without the bass part.

18

say a-dieu, Good-bye, my lov-er good-bye!_____

say a-dieu, Good-bye, my lov-er good-bye!_____

say a-dieu, Good-bye, my lov-er good-bye!_____

A-dieu, Good-bye, my lov-er good-bye! Good-bye.

By-low, my ba-by, By-low, my ba-by,

By-low, my ba-by, By-low, my ba-by,

By-low, ba-by, By-low, my ba-by,

By-low, ba-by, By-low, ba-by,

B-371

BABYLON

TBB
U.I.L. Sight Reading Selection for Classes A and AA (TBB).

ANONYMOUS   THERON KIRK

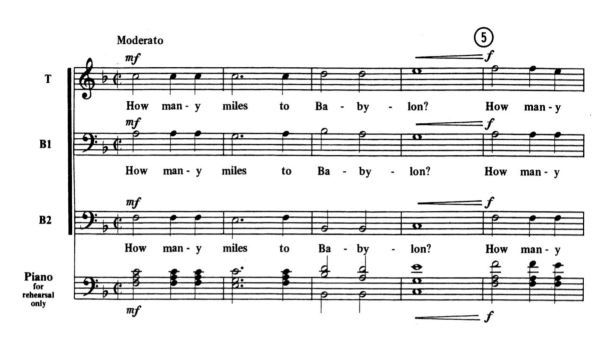

24

B-371

Known Only to God

(TOMB OF THE UNKNOWN SOLDIER)

TTB

U.I.L. Sight Reading Selection for Class AA

CHRISTINA CLAMANN

BOBBY L. SILTMAN

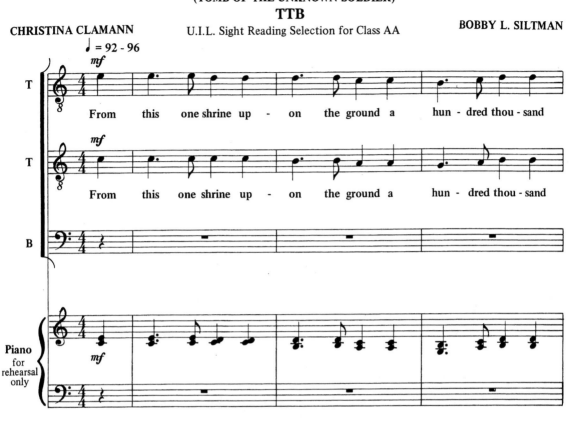

26

pray for peace in oth - er lands.

pray for peace in oth - er lands. Here lies a man who gave of his life.

pray for peace in oth - er lands. Here lies a man who gave of his life.

Loud are his deeds though

Peace was his goal, yes, a world free from strife. Loud are his deeds though

Peace was his goal, yes, a world free from strife. Loud are his deeds though

B-371

28

many more must the lot be cast, un-til man-kind knows sweet peace at last. From

many more must the lot be cast, un-til man-kind knows sweet peace at last. From

man-y more must the lot be cast, un-til man-kind knows sweet peace at last. From

25

rit. *p*

this one shrine up - on the ground a hun - dred thou - sand voic - es sound.

rit. *p*

this one shrine up - on the ground a hun - dred thou - sand voic - es sound.

rit. *p*

this one shrine up - on the ground a hun - dred thou - sand voic - es sound.

rit. *p*

STEAL AWAY
(TTB or TBB)

American Black Spiritual
Arranged by BOBBY L. SILTMAN

32

B-371

CONTENT
(TBB)

ROBERT HERRICK

C. M. SHEARER

34

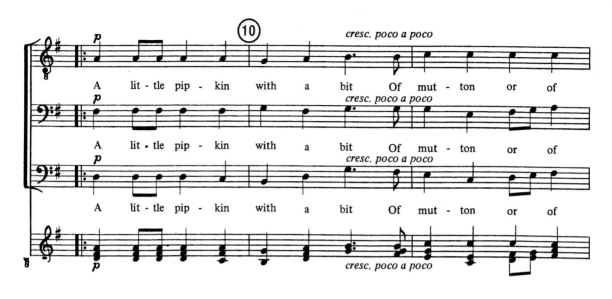

A lit-tle pip-kin with a bit Of mut-ton or of

veal in it, Set on my ta-ble, trou-ble free,

More than a feast con-tent-eth me.

B-371

THE ANGLER'S SONG

U.I.L. Sight Reading Selection, Class AAA Boys (TBB).

WILLIAM BASSE
(11 Century)

C.M. SHEARER

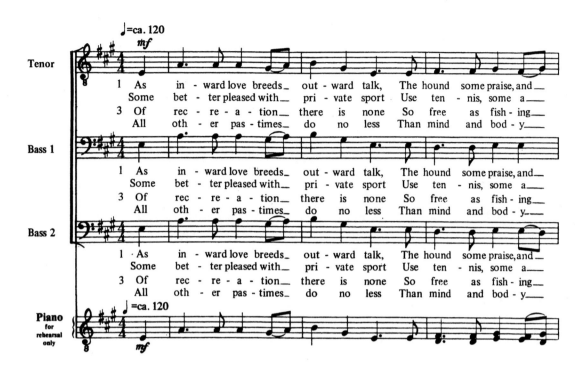

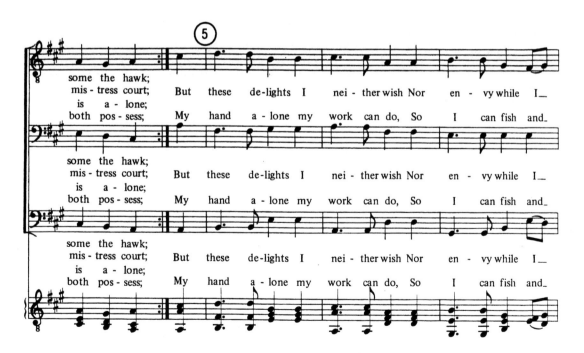

36

B-371

falls in love Is fet - tered in fond Cup - id's snare; My
im - i - tate; In civ - il bounds I fain would keep; And

falls in love Is fet - tered in fond Cup - id's snare; My
im - i - tate; In civ - il bounds I fain would keep; And

falls in love Is fet - tered in fond Cup - id's snare; My
im - i - tate; In civ - il bounds I fain would keep; And

D.C. al Coda
(with repeat)

Coda

an - gle breed me no such care.
for my past of -

fens - es weep.

an - gle breed me no such care.
for my past of -

fens - es weep.

an - gle breed me no such care.
for my past of -

fens - es weep.

LOVE

TBB
U.I.L. Sight Reading Selection for Class AAA (TBB).

SAMUEL BUTLER

THERON KIRK

40

B-371

GREATER LOVE

U.I.L. Sight Reading Selection for Class AAA (TTB)

Words and Music by
B. L. SILTMAN

B-371

42

B-371

do what-so-ev - er com - mand - ed. You are my friend.

do what-so-ev - er com - mand - ed. You are my friend.

do what-so-ev - er com - mand - ed. You are my friend.

This is my com - mand-ment. You shall love one an -

This is my com - mand-ment. You shall love one an -

This is my com - mand-ment. You shall love one an -

SHALL I WASTING IN DESPAIR
(TTBB Choir)

GEORGE WITHER*

C.M. SHEARER

*G. Wither (1588-1667)

48

Come, Let's Begin

**U.I.L. Sight Reading Selection for Class AAA and Class AAAA
and Class AAAAA 2nd groups**

Unknown, 16th cen.

C. M. SHEARER

Come, come, come, let's be-gin to rev-el, rev-el, rev-el it out.

Come, come, come, let's be-gin to rev-el, rev-el, rev-el it out.

Come, come, come, let's be-gin to rev-el, rev-el, rev-el it out.

Come, come, come, let's be-gin to rev-el, rev-el, rev-el it out. And

Come, come, come, let's be-gin to rev-el, rev-el, rev-el it out.

Come, come, come, let's be-gin to rev-el, rev-el, rev-el it out.

tread the hills and vales a - bout, Come, come, let's be-gin to rev-el it

Tread the hills, tread the vales, Come, be - gin to rev - el.

Tread the hills, tread the vales, Come, be - gin to rev - el.

out. Come, come, come, come, let's be-gin to rev-el, rev - el,

Come, come, come, come, come, let's be-gin to rev-el, rev - el,

Come, come, come, come, come, let's be-gin to rev-el, rev-el,

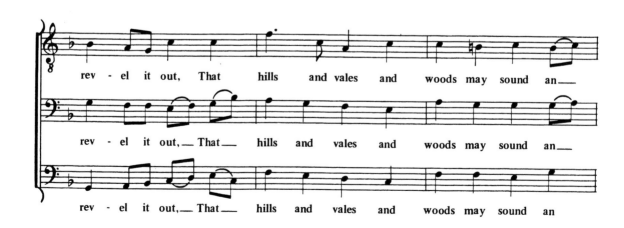

rev - el it out, That hills and vales and woods may sound an

rev - el it out, That hills and vales and woods may sound an

rev - el it out, That hills and vales and woods may sound an

ech - o, an ech - o, an echo, an ech - o. Come,

ech - o, an ech - o, an echo, an ech - o. Come,

ech - o, an ech - o, an echo, an ech - o. Come,

come, let's be - gin to rev - el, rev - el, rev - el it out and sing!

come, let's be - gin to rev - el, rev - el, rev - el it out and sing!

come, let's be - gin to rev - el, rev - el, rev - el it out and sing!

The Gods Have Heard My Vows

U.I.L. Sight Reading Selection for Class AAAA

Unknown, 16th cen.   **C. M. SHEARER**

The gods have heard my vows, My la - dy, whose fair

The gods have heard my vows, My la - dy, whose fair

The gods have heard my vows, My la - dy, whose fair

B-371

54

B-371

LIMERICKS, LIMERICKS, LIMERICKS*

TTBB
U.I.L. Sight Reading Selection for Class AAAA Treble (TTBB).

C.M. SHEARER

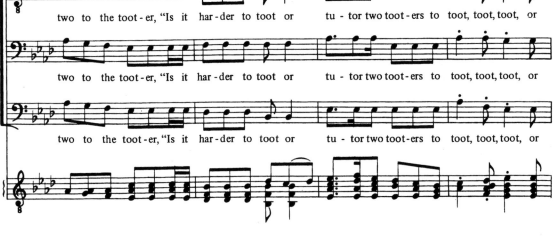

Suggestions for performance: The conductor and chorus are encouraged to add their favorite limerick text for additional verses. This may necessitate a slight change of the rhythms printed. If additional limericks are used, it is suggested that the one printed is sung last. The optional ending is to be sung only with the verse printed if desired.

58

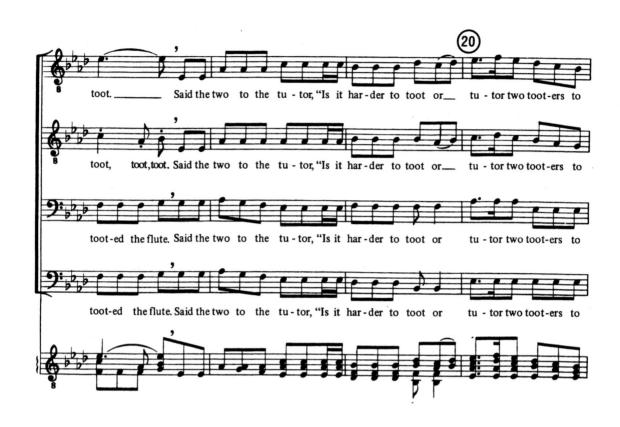

toot. _____ Said the two to the tu-tor, "Is it har-der to toot or___ tu-tor two toot-ers to

toot, toot,toot. Said the two to the tu-tor, "Is it har-der to toot or___ tu-tor two toot-ers to

toot-ed the flute. Said the two to the tu-tor, "Is it har-der to toot or tu-tor two toot-ers to

toot-ed the flute. Said the two to the tu-tor, "Is it har-der to toot or tu-tor two toot-ers to

optional ending

toot, toot, toot, or toot-er two toot-ers to toot?" toot, toot, toot, toot?"

toot, toot, toot, or toot-er two toot-ers to toot?" toot, toot, toot, toot?"

toot, toot, toot, or toot-er two toot-ers to toot?" toot, toot, toot, toot?"

toot, toot, toot, or toot-er two toot-ers to toot?" toot, toot, toot, toot?"

O MISTRESS MINE

SHAKESPEARE

TTBB
U.I.L. Sight Reading Selection for Class AAAAA (TTBB).

THERON KIRK

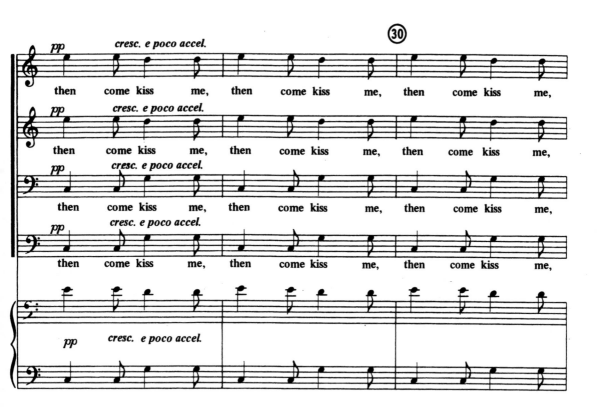

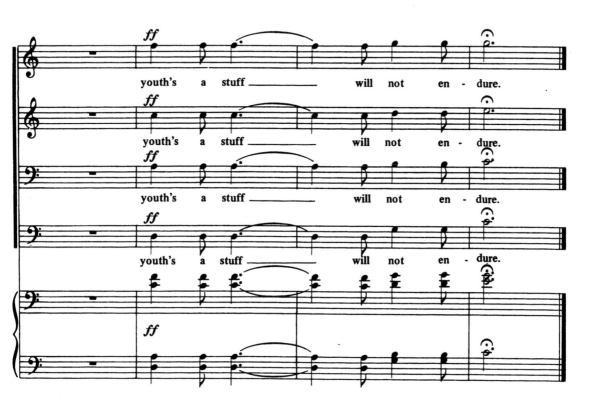

Southern Music
SONGS FOR SIGHT SINGING COLLECTIONS

SONGS FOR SIGHT SINGING *provides a collection of literature for use in the choral classroom. Each selection was composed according to the criteria designed by Texas choral directors and commissioned by the Texas University Interscholastic League for use in its annual sight singing contest. These graded materials were created specifically for young musicians by recognized composers and comprise a valuable resource as they contain many of the problems encountered in sight singing. This collection can be used effectively as a supplement to the daily instructional sight singing program after an approved system (movable "do", fixed "do" or numbers) and a rhythm system are established within the choral curriculum.*

VOLUME 1

edited by Mary Henry, Marilyn Jones and Ruth Whitlock
B370 Songs for Sight Singing Vol. 1: HIGH SCHOOL/ SA
B371 Songs for Sight Singing Vol. 1: HIGH SCHOOL/ TB
B372 Songs for Sight Singing Vol. 1: HIGH SCHOOL/ SATB
B373 Songs for Sight Singing Vol. 1: JUNIOR HIGH/ SA
B374 Songs for Sight Singing Vol. 1: JUNIOR HIGH/ TB
B375 Songs for Sight Singing Vol. 1: JUNIOR HIGH/ SATB
B376 Songs for Sight Singing Vol. 1: JUNIOR HIGH - HIGH SCHOOL/ SAB

VOLUME 2

edited by Mary Henry, Marilyn Jones and Ruth Whitlock
B514 Songs for Sight Singing Vol. 2: HIGH SCHOOL/ SA
B515 Songs for Sight Singing Vol. 2: HIGH SCHOOL/ TB
B516 Songs for Sight Singing Vol. 2: HIGH SCHOOL/ SATB
B517 Songs for Sight Singing Vol. 2: JUNIOR HIGH/ SA
B518 Songs for Sight Singing Vol. 2: JUNIOR HIGH/ TB
B519 Songs for Sight Singing Vol. 2: JUNIOR HIGH/ SATB
B520 Songs for Sight Singing Vol. 2: JUNIOR HIGH - HIGH SCHOOL/ SAB

VOLUME 3

edited by Vivian Munn and Renee Higgins
B557 Songs for Sight Singing Vol. 3: HIGH SCHOOL/ SATB
B558 Songs for Sight Singing Vol. 3: HIGH SCHOOL/ SA
B559 Songs for Sight Singing Vol. 3: HIGH SCHOOL/ TB
B560 Songs for Sight Singing Vol. 3: JUNIOR HIGH - HIGH SCHOOL/ SAB
B561 Songs for Sight Singing Vol. 3: JUNIOR HIGH/ SATB
B562 Songs for Sight Singing Vol. 3: JUNIOR HIGH/ SA
B563 Songs for Sight Singing Vol. 3: JUNIOR HIGH/ TB

Southern
MUSIC
Exclusively Distributed By
HAL•LEONARD
CORPORATION